CALIFORNIA

in words and pictures

BY DENNIS B. FRADIN

ILLUSTRATIONS BY ROBERT ULM

CHILDRENS PRESS ®
CHICAGO

Carmel

Library of Congress Cataloging in Publication Data

Fradin, Dennis.
   California in words and pictures.

   SUMMARY: A brief introduction to the land, history,
cities, industries, and famous sites of the Golden State.
   1. California—Juvenile literature. [California]
I. Ulm, Robert II. Title
F861.3.F72   979.4   76-50600
ISBN 0-516-03905-9

10 11 12 13 14 15 16 17 R 93 92 91 90 89 88

Picture Acknowledgments:
AMERICAN AIRLINES:cover, 2, 23 (above left), 29, 33 (above),
   35 (above)
DEPARTMENT OF THE ARMY—21,41
UNION PACIFIC RAILROAD COLORPHOTO—23, (above), 32, 33 (left)
   35, 37 (top left)
SAN DIEGO CONVENTION AND VISITORS BUREAU—23 (left), 24
SANTA FE RAILWAY—25, 27
DEPT. OF WATER AND POWER, CITY OF LOS ANGELES—26
WIDE WORLD PHOTO—31
U.S. BUEAU OF RECLAMATION—37 (bottom left, above, right)
U.S. DEPT. OF THE INTERIOR: NATIONAL PARK SERVICE PHOTO
   BY FRED E. MANG, JR.—39 (left), 41 (above left and above right),
   42; PHOTO BY W.S. KELLY—39 (above)
CALIFORNIA REDWOOD ASSOCIATION—39 (top left)
COVER PICTURE: Cable car in San Francisco

California (kal • ih • FORN • ya). That was the name of a lovely treasure island in an old Spanish story. Later, Spanish explorers came to a beautiful land. It reminded them of the old story. So they named it California.

Do you know which state has the most people? Which has the greatest fishing and farming? What state makes the most airplanes? And where the biggest and oldest of all living things are found?

As you will see, the answer to all these questions is—California!

Millions of years ago—before there were people—saber-toothed tigers and huge mammoths ruled the land. A lot was happening to that land. There were great earthquakes as mountains rose out of the ground. And for ages of time the lowlands were covered by oceans.

The water dried. The Ice Age came. During this time, huge blocks of ice called glaciers (GLAY • shers) moved down from the north and covered some of the land. Glaciers carved out canyons and smoothed out valleys. Finally the Ice Age ended. The glaciers melted, leaving lakes behind.

Indians were the first people who lived on this land. Lots of Indian tribes lived peacefully for thousands of years. The Indians near the ocean made redwood canoes and fished for salmon. They gathered shells from the beaches and used them for money. The Indians who lived in the forests made baskets and gathered nuts. The mountain Indians lived in caves. You can still see paintings that Indian artists made on cave walls.

The first outsiders were explorers for the far-
away country of Spain. Spain controlled Mexico,
which is just south of California. "Go, see what is
north of Mexico!" ordered the king of Spain.

Juan Cabrillo (huan ka • BREE • yo) was the first explorer. In 1542 he sailed along the California coast and stopped in San Diego (san dee • AY • go) Bay. Cabrillo gave Spanish names to many of the places he saw. But the Indian did not like these outsiders. Three of Cabrillo's men were wounded by Indian arrows. Cabrillo was badly hurt. His men tried to save him, but he died. He is buried in California soil, although no one knows the exact spot.

Later, other Spanish explorers came. The land became part of a huge area controlled by Spain.

Spanish soldiers came. They built forts, called *presidios* (pri • SID • eeyo). Settlers from Spain and Mexico came, also. They built towns, called *pueblos* (PWAY • bloz).

Spanish priests came, too. The priests built missions. Father Junípero Serra (hoo • NAY • perro SAIR • ah) founded the first mission at San Diego in 1769. Over the years, 21 missions were built along the coast. Each mission was one day's ride from the last one. Travelers could ride along a road called the King's Highway and sleep each night at a mission.

The Indians were forced to live at the missions. The Indians had to farm the land, look after the cattle, and put up many of the buildings.

Spain ruled California for hundreds of years. But then Mexico fought a long war with Spain. Mexico won the war and became free of Spain. Now governors from Mexico ruled everyone in California.

In the early 1800's American settlers began going to California. Some were fur trappers—men who caught animals and sold the furs. Others were American families who came to farm this rich land.

It was very, very hard for these Americans to get to California. They traveled in covered wagons which

were pulled by oxen. A group of wagons was called a "wagon train." The trip was thousands of miles from Missouri or Illinois. Sometimes there were no trails. The wagon trains had to cross rivers, deserts, and towering mountains. For food, the people shot buffalo and antelope. Friendly Indians helped the settlers and told them which trail was the best. Other Indians attacked the wagon trains.

Many people died on the way. But most people made it to California!

Better trails were made and more settlers came. The people set up farms and ranches. But they were still ruled by the governors from Mexico.

"We came here ourselves—we want to *rule* ourselves!" said many settlers. "Free California from Mexico! Make it part of the United States of America!"

A soldier, John Frémont (FREE . mont), explored California for the United States army. The United States decided that it wanted this land. Mexico and the United States went to war. John Frémont helped the United States defeat the Mexican army.

In 1848, California became part of the United States. But it wasn't a state yet. It was a territory. About 26,000 people lived here then.

But then something happened which brought thousands and thousands of people to California. Gold was found!

"Gold! California is the golden land! Come to California and get rich!" people cried.

From all over America—from all over the *world*—people came. Some crossed America by covered wagons. Some sailed all the way around South America. Others sailed to Central America,

walked through the jungles, then sailed on to
California. This was the greatest gold rush the
world has ever known. In the year 1849, 80,000 people
came to California.

The gold miners needed places to sleep. They had to buy food and clothes. In places where there were a lot of miners, towns went up. Hangtown and Rich Gulch, Dogtown, Rawhide, and Humbug—these were some of the mining towns that grew across California.

The gold rush made San Francisco grow overnight. Ships carrying supplies and miners sailed every day into San Francisco Bay. Sacramento—near where gold was first found—grew into a big city. Los Angeles also began to grow.

Most often the miners just found gold dust. But sometimes, chunks of gold called nuggets were found. One man picked up a 25-pound nugget. Another man was chasing his cow across a field. He stubbed his toe on a rock. It was made of gold! This was the start of a 80-million-dollar gold mine.

Children found gold. One boy was looking for rocks
for his slingshot. He found a gold nugget that was
worth a thousand dollars!

Very few miners got rich. Most of the miners worked all day just to pay for their food and a place to sleep. In those days, eggs cost the miners three dollars each. A pound of potatoes or onions cost more than ten dollars.

California was a wild, lawless place then. There were many bandits. Rattlesnake Dick, Black Bart, and Three-Fingered Jack were famous badmen.

In 1850 California became the 31st state. The gold started to give out around 1854. But the people stayed! They stayed because they liked California. It was a good place to grow crops. Business was booming in the big cities. By 1860 California had a population of about 380,000. And law and order were coming to California. It was soon safe to raise a family here.

But one thing bothered Californians. They felt cut off from people in the states back East. It took weeks to send a letter by stagecoach.

The young men of the Pony Express carried the mail much faster. When one rider got tired he would hand the mail to a new, fresh rider. The Pony Express brought mail to California in just seven or eight days.

But then telegraph lines reached California. Now Californians could get messages from the East very quickly.

It was still very hard to *get* people and goods to California, however. That was why, in the 1860's, some rich men started a great railroad. This railroad was to go across the country. For six years Chinese, Italian, and Irish workers laid the tracks. At times snow buried the new tracks. Sometimes Indians attacked the workmen. But on May 10, 1869, the railroad was finished. The last spike was driven in a—golden spike! Now people could ride across the United States to California.

In the early 1900's a new kind of treasure was found. This was oil,-"black gold." The United States needed oil to heat houses, to run machines, and also for a new invention—the car. Just like in the Gold Rush, thousands flocked to the California oil fields.

People came to California to build ships, help make airplanes, and work in other kinds of factories.

People went to California to farm the land.

Older people picked the warm Golden State as the place to spend their golden years.

People! People! People! So many came to California that in 1963 it became the state with the most people.

A TRIP THROUGH CALIFORNIA

California is a large state. You'd need to
spend years on a magic carpet to see all
of California. This trip is just going to
take you to *some* of the interesting
places.

Sacramento (sack • rah • MEN • toe) is the
capital. It is near the center of the state.
The dome of the capitol building is made
from California gold.

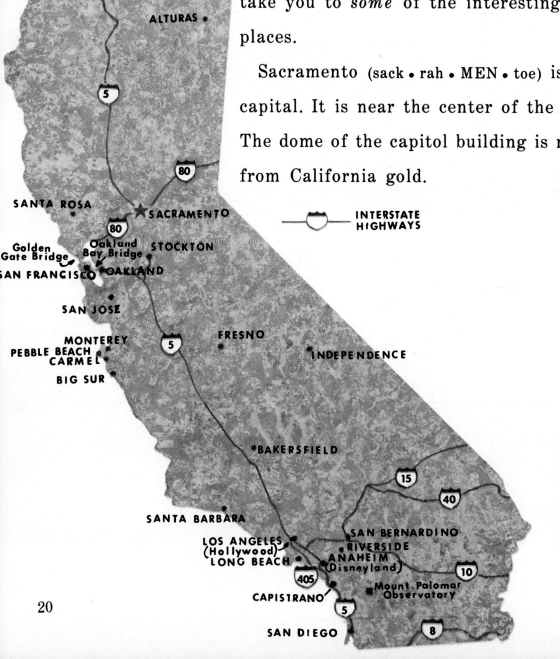

INTERSTATE HIGHWAYS

Left: Nuclear power plant,
Sacramento Municipal Utility District

Above: California state
capitol, Sacramento

Sacramento was founded by John Sutter, who came from Switzerland. Sutter's Fort has been rebuilt to look like it did in 1848, when the first gold was discovered here. Strangely, John Sutter himself did not get rich from the gold. He was a bad businessman, and he died poor.

What would John Sutter think if he saw Sacramento today? Rocket engines are made here now. And fruits and vegetables are packed in factories.

21

Many of California's big cities have been built near the shores of the Pacific Ocean. San Diego, only 16 miles north of Mexico, is a fine place to begin a trip up the coast.

Ships and airplanes are built in San Diego. And there's a good chance that the tuna you eat may have been canned here.

Visit Cabrillo National Monument. It reminds you of Juan Cabrillo, the first explorer in California.

All about the city you are reminded of the days when Spain owned California. Streets and parks have Spanish names. Many of the houses are done in the Spanish style. You can see ruins of the *presidio* (fort) that was built by Spanish soldiers. And the mission has been rebuilt to look just as it did in 1769 when it was built by Father Junípero Serra.

Above: Cabrillo National Monument
Above left: Cabrillo National Monument and park
Left: Giraffes in San Diego Zoo

If you like animals, San Diego is your city. The
San Diego Zoo is often called the world's best zoo.
Here the animals have lots of room. The city's huge
aquarium is called Sea World.

If you like to study the stars, you may want to visit the biggest telescope in the United States, high up on nearby Mount Palomar (PAL • oh • mar). Astronomers have used this telescope to discover stars that are trillions of miles away.

Mount Palomar

San Bernardino Freeway, outside Los Angeles

Los Angeles (loss AN • jel • ess), the biggest city in California, is 130 miles up the coast from San Diego. In the 1980s, Los Angeles became the second largest city in the U.S.

Los Angeles means "City of Angels" in Spanish. It was the second village, or *pueblo*, that the Spanish built in California. In 1781, when it was founded, 44 people lived there. Now the city of Los Angeles has about three million people.

A view of Los Angeles

There are many exciting places in Los Angeles—"L.A." as it is called for short.

Moviemaking is a big business that employs a lot of people. L.A. is also one of the leading airplane-making cities in the country. So you might say that the "City of Angels" has wings! And like San Diego, L.A. is a great fishing port.

Chinatown in Los Angeles

Many different kinds of people live in L.A. There are 450,000 Mexican-Americans. Most of them live in a section of L.A. called the *barrio*, (BARE • e • oh) a Spanish word for "neighborhood." Near City Hall is a Japanese neighborhood called "Little Tokyo." Not far from Little Tokyo is Chinatown. Over half a million black people also live and work in Los Angeles.

In L.A. you must visit the famous La Brea (la Bray • ah) Tar Pits. In 1870 Henry Hancock bought a ranch. He called it Rancho La Brea (Spanish for "tar ranch").

When Los Angeles needed tar to pave the streets, Hancock was offered $20 for each ton of tar. But there was one problem. The tar was filled with thousands of animal bones and teeth!

Scientists came. They said that the bones belonged to animals that lived a million years ago. These animals had gotten stuck in the tar and died.

At the nearby Museum of Natural History you can see these bones.

Outside Los Angeles, visit Disneyland. Go inside a castle or take a make-believe rocket trip to Mars.

Above: Monterey
Right: Carmel

It is 350 miles between Los Angeles and San Francisco. A trip by car can take all day, but it is a lot of fun. The beaches—like Pebble Beach and Big Sur—give you a breathtaking view of the ocean. There are many interesting towns, too. Carmel (kar • MELL) is an old-fashioned town that has no street lights or mail boxes. Another town, Monterey (mon • ter • RAY), was the capital when Spain and Mexico ruled California.

29

San Francisco (san fran • SISS • koh) is a city that has survived many bad times. Half a dozen times, before 1900, San Francisco had great fires. Then, on April 18, 1906, came the biggest disaster of all. A great earthquake shook San Francisco. An earthquake is caused when rocks move far below the surface of the Earth. The rocks move in certain weak points, called *faults*. A big fault—the San Andreas (san an • DRAY • as) Fault—stretches down most of California's coast.

The 1906 quake started out with a low rumbling sound. Then buildings began to shake. The rumbling became a roar. The ground trembled and great cracks opened in the earth. Buildings fell. After the quake the city caught fire. The fires raged for three days. When the fires were finally out, much of San Francisco lay in ruins. Over 450 people had been killed.

A view of San Francisco after the earthquake

But the people of San Francisco did not despair. "We'll build a new, greater city!" they said.

And this is just what they did! Look at Downtown San Francisco today. It is one of the leading banking areas in the world.

Cable car turnaround in Aquatic Park, San Francisco

San Francisco is often called the "City of Hills." Long ago, horses had a hard time pulling carriages up the hills. So, in 1873, Andrew Hallidie invented the cable car. "Cables, under the street, will pull the cars along," said Hallidie. When he tested his first cable car, people came to laugh. But they stopped laughing when the thing worked!

Take a cable car to Nob Hill, where the richest people in San Francisco used to live. Near Nob Hill are the bright lights of Chinatown. About 32,000 Chinese people live in San Francisco—more than in any other American city. More than 12,000 Japanese-Americans also live here.

You can go by cable car to Fisherman's Wharf. The boats keep coming in, loaded with fish. This is the place to eat good fish.

Left: Fisherman's Wharf
Above: The Union Club, Nob Hill

San Francisco is built right next to a thumb-shaped part of the Pacific Ocean called the San Francisco Bay.

In 1937 a huge bridge was built which connected San Francisco to the northern part of California. This is the famous Golden Gate Bridge. It is over a mile long and, when you ride over it, you are 20-stories above the water.

A boat tour will take you right under the Golden Gate Bridge. On the boat ride you will pass Seal Rocks, where seals play in the sun. In the Bay itself you can see Alcatraz (AL • ka • traz) Island, where dangerous prisoners used to be kept. Another "island," Treasure Island, was man-made. It was used for a World's Fair in 1939 and 1940.

Top: Cliff House and Seal Rocks

Left: Golden Gate Bridge

Above: Alcatraz

East of San Francisco lies the Central Valley. This is a huge farming area 500 miles long and 100 miles wide. Millions of years ago, the valley was covered by oceans. The oceans dried, leaving a rich layer of soil. Do you like grapes, olives, lemons, peaches, and pears? These and almost every kind of crop you can think of are grown in the Central Valley.

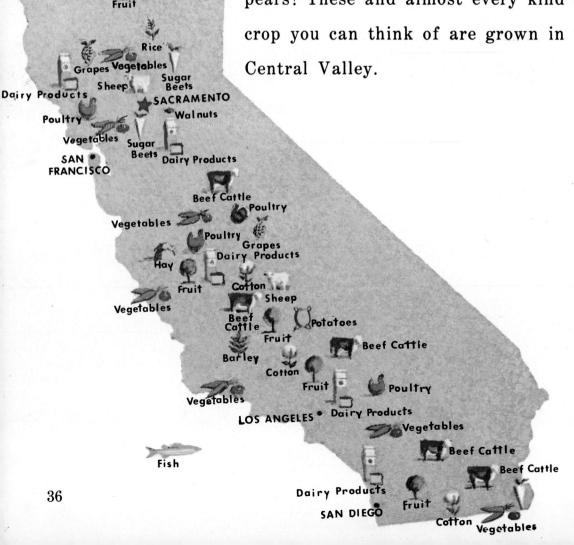

Fruit

Rice

Grapes Vegetables

Sheep

Sugar Beets

Dairy Products

SACRAMENTO

Poultry

Walnuts

Vegetables

Sugar Beets

SAN FRANCISCO

Dairy Products

Beef Cattle

Poultry

Vegetables

Poultry

Grapes

Dairy Products

Hay

Fruit

Cotton

Sheep

Vegetables

Beef Cattle

Potatoes

Fruit

Beef Cattle

Barley

Cotton

Fruit

Poultry

Vegetables

Dairy Products

LOS ANGELES

Vegetables

Fish

Beef Cattle

Beef Cattle

Dairy Products

SAN DIEGO

Fruit

Cotton

Vegetables

Top left: Wine grapes,
Napa Valley

Bottom left: Tomato harvest,
Central Valley

Above: Onion harvest,
Central Valley

Right: Cantaloupes,
Central Valley

But the Central Valley and other parts of California have a water problem. There is not enough rainfall. So water is brought from far away. How is this done? The water flows in long canals, called *aqueducts* (AK • wa • dukts), until it reaches the farmland where it is needed.

Many kinds of animals are raised by California ranchers. Beef cattle, dairy cows, sheep, hogs, and poultry provide food for people.

Forests cover over a third of California. On the Pacific Coast are the redwood forests. Redwoods are the *tallest* living things on Earth.

In the eastern part of the state grow the fat cousins of the redwoods—the giant sequoias (si • KWOI • ah). Giant sequoias are not as tall as the redwoods, but they are much fatter. They are the *very largest* living things on Earth.

Redwoods and giant sequoias live for thousands of years. But the bristlecone pines live longer. At Ancient Bristlecone Pine Forest there are trees that are 4600 years old. They were alive when the pyramids of Egypt were being built.

Top left: Redwood trees in Big River area

Bottom left: General Sherman tree-272 feet high, 100 feet round

Stretching for 400 miles along California's eastern edge are the Sierra Nevadas (see • AIR • ah neh • VAH • dahs)—the highest mountain range in the United States. As mountains go, the Sierra Nevadas are very young. It was only a million years ago that they were pushed out of the Earth.

Yosemite (yo • SEM • ih • te) National Park is in the Sierra Nevadas. There are lots of waterfalls here, including Ribbon Falls, the highest in North America. Yosemite Park also has lakes, canyons, mountains, and forests of giant sequoias. This park was named for the Indians who once lived in the area.

Above left: Bridal Veil Falls, Yosemite National Park

Above right: Yosemite National Park

Left: Rugged snow peaks of the Sierra Nevada

Death Valley

California's Death Valley got its name in 1849. That year thirty gold miners tried to cross the desert. Eighteen of them died of thirst. Those who made it through called it "the valley of death."

The desert sand dunes may look pretty from a car. But you wouldn't want to walk in this desert during a summer day. The temperature in Death Valley often gets up to 120°.

A large number of wild animals live in California. Wildcats, beavers, elk, bears, and deer roam the forests and mountains. Sea lions, sea otters, and fur seals live in the waters off the coast. Rattlesnakes, coyotes, and lizards live in the deserts.

One of the most interesting animals anywhere is the California sea otter. Sea otters are very smart. They take stones from the bottom of the ocean and use them to open crabs and clams.

Sadly, some of California's wild animals have been killed off completely. There are no more California grizzly bears. And the largest bird in North America, the California condor, is in danger.

California is home to the famous swallows of Capistrano (cap • iss • TRAH • no). Every year, on October 23, the swallows leave the mission at Capistrano and fly south for the winter. And every year, on March 19, they return to Capistrano. No one knows how these birds keep such a good calendar in their heads. But, like a lot of people, they keep coming back to California!

A land rich in Spanish history . . .

The land of the greatest gold rush . . .

Home of moviemaking . . . Disneyland . . . the Golden Gate Bridge . . .

The leader in farming . . . fishing . . . and people . . .

This is California, the Golden State!

Facts About CALIFORNIA

Area—158,693 square miles
Highest Point—14,494 feet above sea level (Mount Whitney)
Lowest Point—282 feet below sea level (Death Valley)
Hottest Recorded Temperature—134° (in 1913, in Death Valley; the
        hottest it's ever been anywhere in
        U.S.)
Coldest Recorded Temperature—minus 45° (in 1937, at Boca)
Statehood—31st state, September 9, 1850
Capital—Sacramento (1854)
Counties—58
U.S. Senators—2
U.S. Representatives—45
Electoral Votes—47
State Senators—40
State Assemblymen—80
State Song—"I Love You, California," by F.B. Silverwood and A.F.
        Frankenstein
State Motto—*Eureka* (Greek for "I have found it")
Nickname—Golden State
State Seal—Adopted in 1849
State Flag—Adopted in 1911
Principal Rivers—Sacramento (382 miles long)
        San Joaquin (350 miles long)
        Colorado (on border between southern California
        and Arizona)
        Dams—Oroville, San Luis, Castaic, Shasta
        Waterfalls—Ribbon Falls (1,612 feet, highest in
        North America)
        Upper Yosemite Falls (1,430 feet)
        and Lower Yosemite Falls (320 feet)
        Silverstrand (1,170 feet)
        Feather Falls (640 feet)
        Bridalveil (620 feet)
        Deserts—Mohave (about 1500 square miles)
        Colorado
        Death Valley
        Lakes—About 8000 within the state
        Harbors—San Francisco Bay, San Diego Bay,
        Humboldt Bay, Monterey Bay

CALIFORNIA REPUBLIC

STATE FLAG

STATE SEAL

STATE BIRD
(California Valley Quail)

STATE FLOWER
(Golden Poppy)

STATE TREE
(California Redwood)

State Symbols—Tree: California redwoods
Bird: California valley quail
Animal: California grizzly bear
Fish: California golden trout
Colors: Blue and gold

Farm Products—Grapes, oranges, lettuce, tomatoes, peaches plums, dates, figs, lemons, olives, avocados, cantaloupes, pears, apricots, almonds, cotton, beef cattle, milk, eggs

Fishing—Tuna, salmon, oysters, abalone, crabs, flounder, mackeral, sea bass, swordfish, lobsters, shrimps

Mining—Petroleum, natural gas, boron, mercury, gypsum, gold, copper, silver, talc, zinc

Manufacturing Products—Airplanes, automobiles, wine, canning of food, electrical equipment, machinery

Population—1980 census: 23,667,826 (1985 estimate: 26,365,000)

Population Density—139 persons per square mile (1980 census)

Major Cities	1980 Census	1986 Estimate
Los Angeles	2,968,579	3,298,200
San Diego	875,538	1,035,900
San Francisco	678,974	738,100
San Jose	629,402	715,100
Oakland	339,337	363,500

California History

1542—Juan Cabrillo explores California's coast for Spain

1579—Sir Francis Drake of England explores California

1602—Vizcaíno explores California for Spain

1769—Father Junípero Serra founds the first California mission, near San Diego

1769—San Francisco Bay discovered by Spanish explorer Portolá

1776—San Francisco founded

1781—Pueblo of Los Angeles is founded

1812—Russian fur traders build Fort Ross

1826—California controlled by Mexico

1826—Jedediah Smith, a fur trapper, becomes first American to go overland to California

1829—"Old Spanish Trail" opened, connecting Santa Fe and Los Angeles

1841—First "wagon train" arrives in California

1846—U.S. and Mexico go to war

1848—California becomes U.S. territory by Treaty of Guadalupe Hidalgo

1849—Gold Rush

1850—California becomes the 31st state, on September 9

1850—First public school in state opened in San Francisco

1851—Yosemite Park area explored by Major James Savage

1854—Sacramento becomes the capital

1856—State's first public high school opened in San Francisco

1861—Telegraph connects California to East
1865—Civil War ends
1869—Golden spike driven in as
       transcontinental railroad is completed
1873—Andrew Hallidie invents cable car in
       San Francisco
1874—Capitol building completed in
       Sacramento
1890—First Rose Parade at Pasadena
1892—Oil found in Los Angeles
1906—San Francisco earthquake and fire;
       450 people die
1907—First professional film made in California
1914—Panama Canal opens, making it
       easier to sail from eastern U.S. to California
1915—World's Fair held at San Francisco and San Diego
1917—U.S. enters World War I; California
       becomes shipbuilding center
1917—Lassen Volcano erupts
1925—Earthquake destroys much of
       Santa Barbara
1936—Dinosaur bones found near Patterson
1936—San Francisco-Oakland Bay Bridge
       opened
1937—Central Valley Water Project begun
1939-40—Golden Gate International
       Exposition held on Treasure
       Island
1941—U.S. enter World War II; California
       is center for building airplanes and ships
1945—Shasta Dam completed
1945—United Nations begun in San Francisco
1948—Largest telescope in U.S. completed
       at Mount Palomar
1955—Disneyland opens at Anaheim
1963—California becomes state with the most people
1968—Richard Nixon is elected 37th President
1971—Earthquake in Los Angeles area kills 64
1983—Severe earthquake centering at Coalinga
1984—Olympic Games are held in Los Angeles
1987—Earthquake in Los Angeles area measures 6.1 on Richter Scale

About the Author:

Dennis Fradin attended Northwestern University on a creative writing scholarship and was graduated in 1967. While still at Northwestern, he published his first stories in *Ingenue* magazine and also won a prize in *Seventeen's* short story competition. A prolific writer, Dennis Fradin has been regularly publishing stories in such diverse places as *The Saturday Evening Post, Scholastic, National Humane Review, Midwest,* and *The Teaching Paper.* He has also scripted several educational films. Since 1970 he has taught second grade reading in a Chicago school—a rewarding job, which, the author says, "provides a captive audience on whom I test my children's stories." Married and the father of two children, Dennis Fradin spends his free time with his family or playing a myriad of sports and games with his childhood chums.

About the Artist:

Robert Ulm, a Chicago resident, has been an advertising and editorial artist in both New York and Chicago. Mr. Ulm is a successful painter as well as an illustrator. In his spare time he enjoys fishing and playing tennis.